I0815583

A Day in the Life of a Grizzly Bear

Julie Murray

Abdo Kids Junior
is an Imprint of Abdo Kids
abdobooks.com

abdobooks.com

Published by Abdo Kids, a division of ABDO, P.O. Box 398166, Minneapolis, Minnesota 55439.

Abdo Kids Junior™ is a trademark and logo of Abdo Kids.

Printed in the United States of America, North Mankato, Minnesota.

102025

012026

Photo Credits: Getty Images, Shutterstock

Production Contributors: Teddy Borth, Jennie Forsberg, Grace Hansen

Design Contributors: Candice Keimig, Pakou Moua

Library of Congress Control Number: 2025936504

Publisher's Cataloging-in-Publication Data

Names: Murray, Julie, author.

Title: A day in the life of a grizzly bear / by Julie Murray

Description: Minneapolis, Minnesota : Abdo Kids, 2026 | Series: A day in the life of an animal | Includes online resources and index.

Identifiers: ISBN 9798384907305 (lib. bdg.) | ISBN 9798384908005 (ebook) | ISBN 9798384908357 (read-to-me ebook)

Subjects: LCSH: Grizzly bear--Juvenile literature. | Bears--Juvenile literature. | Bears--Behavior--Juvenile literature. | Predatory animals--Juvenile literature. | Animal behavior--Juvenile literature. | Zoology--Juvenile literature.

Classification: DDC 599.784--dc23

Table of Contents

A Grizzly Bear's Day

It is **dawn**. The grizzly bear wakes.

It comes out of the **brush**.

It **roams** the land.

It looks for food.

The grizzly bear finds some berries to eat.

It digs in the ground.

It eats the plant roots.

The sun is hot. The grizzly bear finds a cool spot to rest.

It is hungry *again*! It walks to the river.

The salmon jump. The grizzly bear catches one in its mouth.

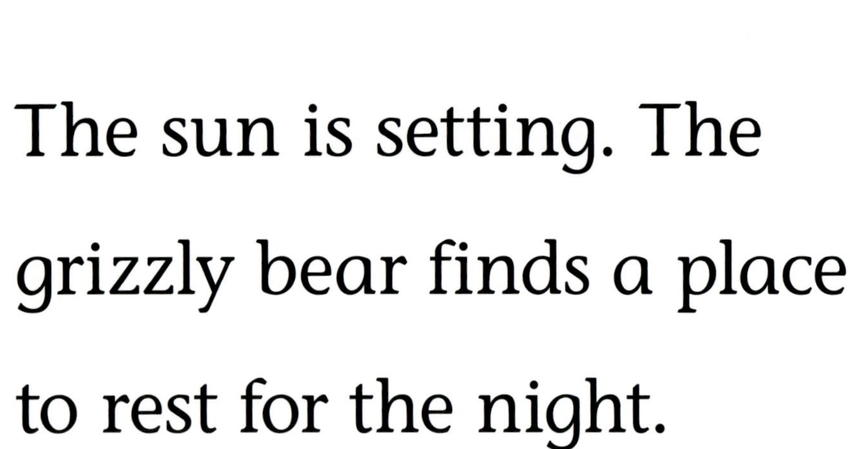

The sun is setting. The grizzly bear finds a place to rest for the night.

Grizzly Bear Facts

Can live up to 25 years in the wild

Can weigh 900 pounds (408 kg)

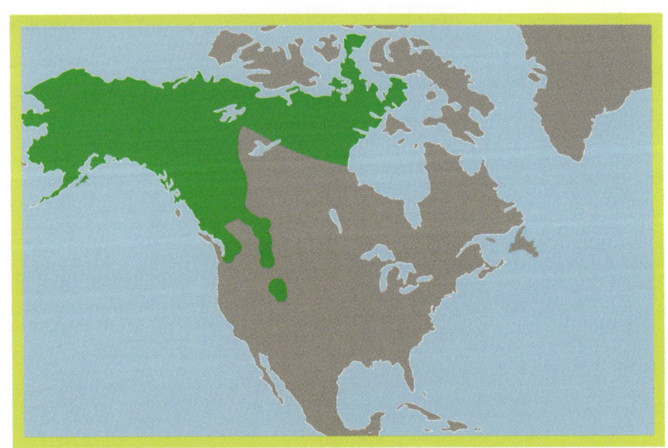

Found in northwestern North America

Hump on its back is muscle for digging

Glossary

brush
a thick group of small trees, shrubs, or bushes growing together.

dawn
the first daylight that appears in the morning.

roam
to move purposefully through a wide area.

Index

Visit **abdokids.com** to access crafts, games, videos, and more!

Use Abdo Kids code

AAK7305

or scan this QR code!